Put each word into the correct sentence.

vaults   basement   rickety   footings   buggy
operator   sett   buskers   bunker

We parked our car in the .... car park and took the lift up to Dad's office.

The babysitter put the bag, nappies and coats in the

....

There are precious documents locked in the .... under the museum.

We listened to two .... playing the violin whilst we waited for Tom.

Under most buildings there are .... underneath the ground's surface.

The machine .... moved the digger carefully.

Rabbits live in a warren; badgers live in a ....

The President was taken to a secret .... to keep her safe.

The only way to cross the gorge was over a .... bridge that swayed in the wind.

Read 'Under My Feet'. Record your thoughts about each of the three questions in the spaces below.

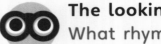

The looking question is ...
What rhyming patterns can you find in the poem?

The clue question is ...
How does the narrator feel about the underground world?

The thinking question is ...
How important is the world under your feet?

Do you have any questions? Write them here.

Think about the conversations you have had about this text. What more have you learned? Complete the activities below.

Imagine you are standing in a busy city: what is beneath your feet?

Discuss which items in the poem are unwanted, which are useful and which are treasure.

Describe an underground place that is not in the poem.

Describe what the people in the underground train might think of the world above them. Write a verse called 'Above My Head'.

Use the space below to list some things above them as they go under streets, houses, parks, buildings and shops.

Write your best ideas as a four line verse in the space below. It doesn't need to rhyme.

Feedback

Use the bold words to write your own sentences in the spaces below.

On the very first day, a human left leg bone was found in the first **trench**.

The Richard III Society is **dedicated** to researching Richard and finding out what sort of king he really was.

There was no **evidence** that Richard's remains had been dug up in the 1500s and thrown into the River Soar.

Do you know what the words below mean? Record your thoughts about each meaning, then look up the words in a dictionary.

I think this word means ...

The definition in the dictionary is ...

osteologist

reputation

fund (verb)

choir of a church (place)

archaeologist

Read pages 2 to 5 of *The King in the Car Park*. Record your thoughts about each of the three questions in the spaces below.

The looking question is ...
How did Philippa Langley find Richard III's body?

The clue question is ...
Why did Philippa Langley want to find Richard III's remains?

The thinking question is ...
Why do we want to find out about the past?

Do you have any questions? Write them here.

Think about the conversations you have had about this text. What more have you learned? Complete the activities below.

Speculate on what each member of the team did for the project.

Explore reasons why Richard III's body wasn't buried properly.

Discuss why people care what happens to someone's body after they die.

Imagine you are at the burial of King Richard III in 1485. What happens? Write your answer below. Underline evidence in the text to support your answer.

3. When the team uncovered the rest of Skeleton 1, they saw that the grave had been dug in a hurry. It was uneven and not very deep.

4. Jo Appleby uncovered the skull and saw that there was damage that could have been inflicted in battle.

5. As digging continued the team realised that Skeleton 1 lay in the choir of a church.

Feedback

Look at the pictures and the words, then look up the words in the dictionary. What do they mean? Write a definition in your own words in the spaces below.

DNA

My Notes

My Notes

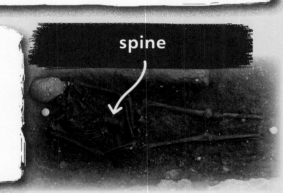

spine

emblem

My Notes

My Notes

protein

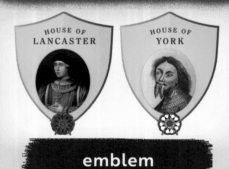

conflict

My Notes

What can you find out about the Wars of the Roses? Complete the activities below.

Who were the two sides in the Wars?

Name three people who were important in the Wars.

Wars of the Roses

When did the Wars of the Roses start and end?

How did the Wars of the Roses end?

Read pages 6 to 11 of *The King in the Car Park*. Record your thoughts about each of the three questions in the spaces below.

The looking question is ...
How did scientists prove that Skeleton I was Richard III?

The clue question is ...
What sort of person was Richard as a young man?

The thinking question is ...
What did a person need in order to become King?

Do you have any questions? Write them here.

Think about the conversations you have had about this text. What more have you learned? Complete the activities below.

Argue that who your parents were was more important in the 15th century than it is now.

Argue that Richard had the skills needed to be a good king.

Describe how you would feel if you were forced to fight for Edward IV.

Imagine you are interviewing Richard about the death of his brother, Edward IV. What questions would you ask? Write three questions on the clipboard below.

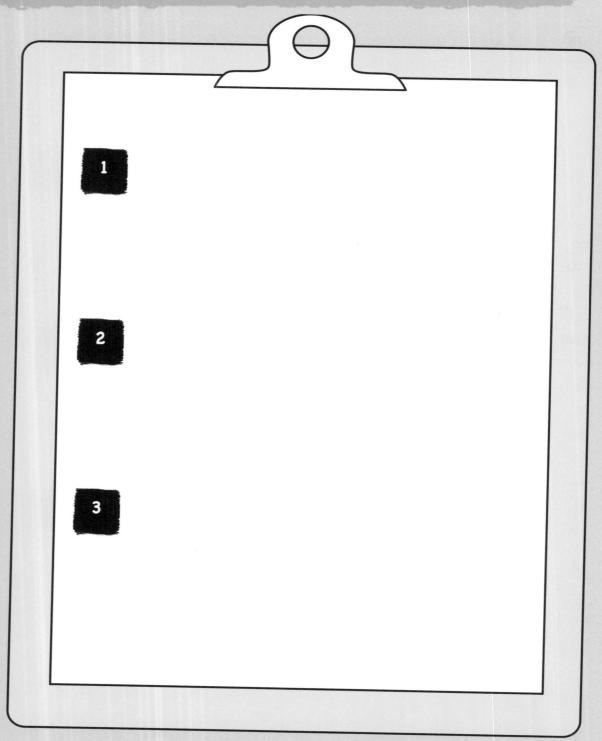

1

2

3

Feedback

What can you find out about the Tower of London? Complete the activities below.

Draw a picture of the Tower of London.

What was the Tower of London for?

Tower of London

Name someone famous who died there.

What would you find there now?

Can you remember these words from pages 6 to 11?
Write two sentences using each word in the spaces below.

spine

DNA

protein

conflict

Read pages 12 to 17 of *The King in the Car Park*. Record your thoughts about each of the three questions in the spaces below.

The looking question is ...
What happened to the two sons of Edward IV after he died?

The clue question is ...
Did Henry Tudor have a better claim to the throne than Richard III?

The thinking question is ...
Which is more important: a strong claim or the ability to rule?

Do you have any questions? Write them here.

Think about the conversations you have had about this text. What more have you learned? Complete the activity below.

Argue whether a battle is a good or bad way to choose a king.

Summarise what happened in the Wars of the Roses, explaining the flow of kings from Henry VI's reign to Richard III's death, using the flowchart below.

Henry VI versus Richard Duke of York (Richard III's father).

Richard's brother Edward becomes King Edward IV.

Edward IV dies; his son becomes King Edward V at 12 years old.

Richard is Lord Protector; the princes are moved to the Tower of London.

King Richard III versus Henry Tudor.

The Battle of Bosworth; Richard III dies.

Feedback

Read the text and complete the activities below.

When Scarlett was accused of writing on the wall in the toilet, I was shocked. I knew it wasn't true and decided that someone must have been plotting to get Scarlett into trouble. I immediately went on a mission to clear her name. First, I organised a petition to have her case heard by the School Council. They agreed that there was no evidence and her reputation was saved.

Find and write down the word that means "planning" or "scheming".

Find and write down the word that means "quest" or "undertaking".

Find and write down the word that means "a collection of signatures supporting a request".

Draw lines to match the bold word in each sentence to the word or phrase which is closest in meaning. Look up any words you don't know in a dictionary.

Raphael sat outside the headteacher's office **hunched** over with shame.

Sadly, the flowers I'd planted **withered** and died whilst we were on our summer holidays.

Jasmine said that her mother was a princess but it was pure **invention**.

Scientists carried out tests on the fossils to **establish** how old they were.

Most of the **descendants** of Flora MacDonald have red hair.

After the diamond necklace was removed, the body was **reinterred** in the graveyard.

All the way back home, Mum and Dad **debated** whose fault it was that we forgot the cake.

Everyone dressed up in carnival costumes and joined the **procession** through the town.

shrivelled

reburied

discussed or argued

bent over

parade

something made up

relatives that live after you

prove

Read from page 18 to the end of *The King in the Car Park*. Record your thoughts about each of the three questions in the spaces below.

The looking question is ...
What burial places for Richard III were considered?

The clue question is ...
Why was Richard III buried in such a grand way?

The thinking question is ...
Do you think Richard III deserved a grand burial?

Do you have any questions? Write them here.

Think about the conversations you have had about this text. What more have you learned? Complete the activity below.

Explore the effect of having a bad reputation.

What do we know about Richard III? Write three words to describe Richard III and explain why you chose those words in the spaces provided.

I think Richard III was ...

I think this because ...

I think Richard III was ...

I think this because ...

I think Richard III was ...

I think this because ...

Feedback

What can you find out about the *Titanic*? Complete the activities below.

Find out an interesting or unusual fact about the *Titanic*. Write it here.

When and where was the *Titanic* built?

The *Titanic*

Why is the *Titanic* famous?

What does the word "titanic" mean? Look it up in the dictionary and write the definition here.

Look at the pictures and the words, then look up the words in the dictionary. What do they mean? Write a definition in your own words in the spaces below.

harbour

My Notes

My Notes

board

My Notes

sink

My Notes

voyage

parted

My Notes

Read Chapter 1 of *Below Deck: A Titanic Story*. Record your thoughts about each of the three questions in the spaces below.

The looking question is ...
What words does the author use to describe the *Titanic*?

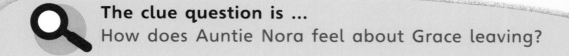

The clue question is ...
How does Auntie Nora feel about Grace leaving?

? **The thinking question is ...**
What would it be like to move to another country?

Do you have any questions? Write them here.

Think about the conversations you have had about this text. What more have you learned? Complete the activities below.

Describe the *Titanic* and what you know about it.

Explain why Auntie Nora is sending Grace to America, even though she is sad to see her go. Use evidence from the text.

Imagine you are travelling to a different country to live. How would you feel and why?

Imagine you are interviewing Grace on the harbour side about her voyage on the *Titanic*. What questions would you ask? Write three questions on the clipboard below.

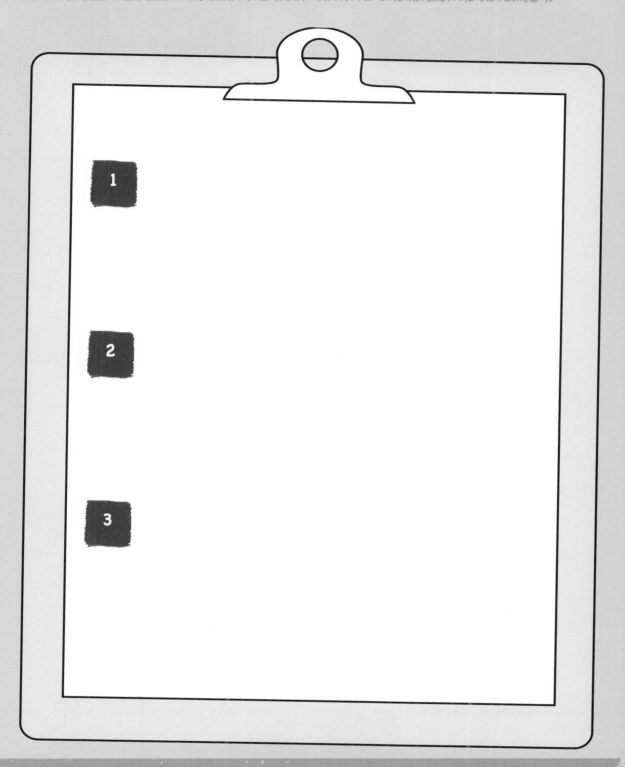

1

2

3

Feedback

Do you know what the words below mean?
Record your thoughts about each meaning,
then look up the words in a dictionary.

I think this
word means ...

The definition in
the dictionary is ...

longingly

glimpse

steward

voyage

curious

Which words or phrases have a similar meaning to the focus word? Write them in the spaces below.

cramped

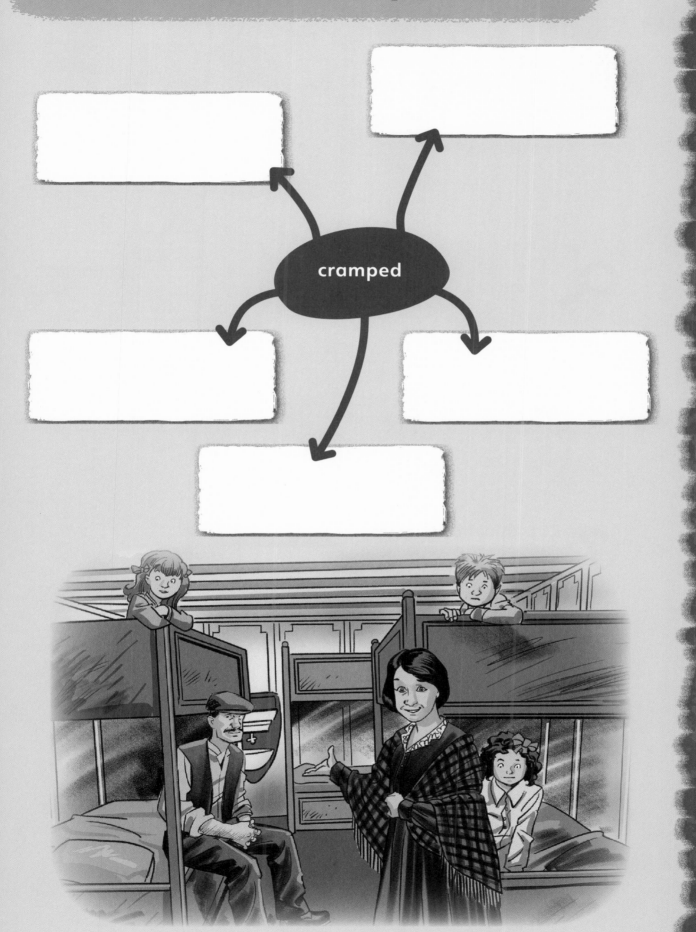

Read Chapter 2 of *Below Deck: A Titanic Story*. Record your thoughts about each of the three questions in the spaces below.

 The looking question is ...
What was it like aboard the *Titanic*?

 The clue question is ...
What did Grace think of first class?

 The thinking question is ...
Why do you think the boys stole the food?

Do you have any questions? Write them here.

Think about the conversations you have had about this text. What more have you learned? Complete the activities below.

Describe what it would feel like to be aboard the *Titanic*.

Argue it is not fair that Grace isn't allowed in the first-class areas.

Discuss if it is wrong to steal.

Imagine you are on the *Titanic*. What can you smell, touch, hear, taste and see? Draw or write your answers in the spaces below.

I can see ...

I can taste ...

I can hear ...

I can smell ...

I can touch ...

Feedback

Put each word into the correct sentence.

thieves accusing accent scowling fortune
pointedly interfered blushing

Some .... stole my friend's favourite purse.

My sister was given a diamond ring, which must have cost a .... to buy.

The headteacher paused .... in the middle of her sentence.

The children .... in the investigation.

The new boy has an .... I don't recognise.

The girl, who lives next door, was .... at me through the window.

Are you .... me of cheating in the spelling test?

My cousin's cheeks were bright red because he was

....

Use the bold words to write your own sentences in the spaces below.

Grace **realised** he and the woman must be the girl's parents.

Grace turned to her, suddenly feeling **uncomfortable** in her patched dress and scuffed old shoes.

"Go away," he **hissed** at her.

The girl pointed an **accusing** finger at Grace.

Read Chapter 3 of *Below Deck: A Titanic Story*. Record your thoughts about each of the three questions in the spaces below.

The looking question is ...
How is Grace feeling about travelling on the *Titanic* at the end of Chapter 3?

The clue question is ...
What similarities and differences are there between Grace and Catherine?

The thinking question is ...
Do you think Catherine was helping or interfering?

Do you have any questions? Write them here.

Think about the conversations you have had about this text. What more have you learned? Complete the activity below.

What is Grace enjoying about being on the *Titanic*, and what doesn't she like?

What do we know about Grace? Write three words to describe Grace and explain why you chose those words in the spaces provided.

I think Grace is ...

I think this because ...

I think Grace is ...

I think this because ...

I think Grace is ...

I think this because ...

Feedback

Change each word so that it fits in the sentences. Write your answers in the spaces provided.

uncontrollably

The robot was out of ....

When the fire alarm went off, the class walked in an .... manner.

The monkeys at the safari park were .... ,

unsinkable

The newspapers had said that the *Titanic* could not .... ,

Passengers on the lifeboats watched as the *Titanic* .... ,

I had a .... feeling that something bad was about to happen.

separated

We travelled to the party .... ,

The twins were always together. They were .... ,

My brother and I have .... bedrooms.

42

Can you remember these words from Chapter 3? Write two sentences using each word in the spaces below.

interfered

accusing

fortune

hissed

Read Chapter 4 of *Below Deck: A Titanic story*. Record your thoughts about each of the three questions in the spaces below.

The looking question is ...
What was it like on the ship after it hit the iceberg?

The clue question is ...
Why did Grace go back inside the ship?

The thinking question is ...
Does Grace forgive Catherine for getting her into trouble?

Do you have any questions? Write them here.

Think about the conversations you have had about this text. What more have you learned? Complete the activities below.

Imagine you are Grace trying to find her cabin while the ship sinks. How would you feel?

Imagine you were in Grace's situation; would you have helped Catherine? Explain why or why not.

What would you rescue from a sinking ship? Describe the items that are most special to you and explain why.

What do you think will happen next? Write your prediction in the space below.

I predict ...

Feedback

Read the text and complete the activities below.

Luke flopped on the sofa with a big smile. He was exhausted after a week on school camp! He had walked over creaking and groaning rope bridges suspended amongst the trees and stumbled through woodland areas on a midnight walk. The expression on Luke's face at the top of the abseiling tower had said it all – he had been terrified! But his cheery, excitable friends had jostled him along throughout the week and Luke had had an amazing time!

Find and copy the word that means "scared".

Find and copy the words that show the rope bridges were not stable.

Which word tells you Luke was feeling tired?

Which words or phrases have a similar meaning to the focus word? Write them in the spaces below.

agony

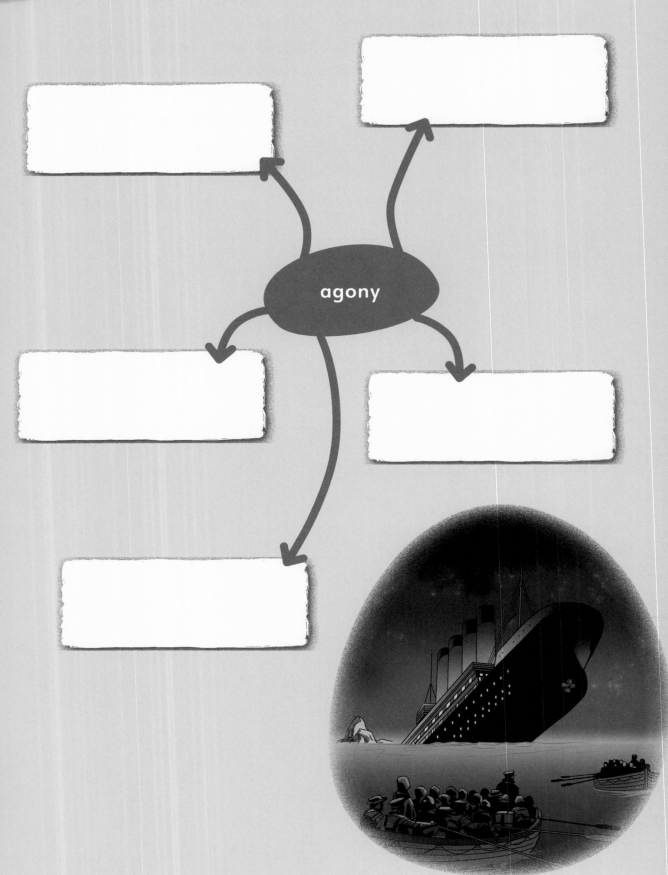

Read Chapter 5 of *Below Deck: A Titanic Story*. Record your thoughts about each of the three questions in the spaces below.

The looking question is ...
Can you find words and phrases the author has used to describe the sinking boat?

The clue question is ...
What are Catherine's strengths and weaknesses?

The thinking question is ...
Should anyone be allowed on the lifeboat regardless of their ticket type?

Do you have any questions? Write them here.

Think about the conversations you have had about this text. What more have you learned? Complete the activities below.

Explain how the author describes the setting aboard the *Titanic* in this chapter.

Explore Catherine's personality using evidence from the text.

Justify the crew member's decision to stop Grace boarding the lifeboat.

Fill in the graph to give each chapter a mark out of 10. Write your reasons for these marks in the space below.

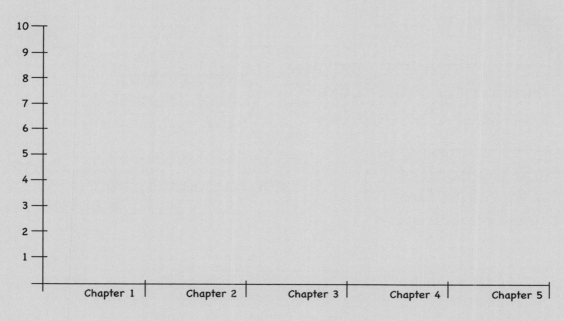

Reading Goals

This term I aim to ...

Find a new author I like!

Read a play with friends!

Read the book of my favourite film!

Learn a poem by heart!

Group Discussion Rules

- We will listen carefully to the person who is speaking

- Everyone should have a chance to speak

- We will give reasons for our ideas

- We can ask others for reasons if they don't say them

- **We can agree and disagree politely with each other**

- We will respect each other's ideas and opinions

- We will share all the information in the group

- We will try to reach an agreement together if we can

Add any other group discussion rules your class or group has decided on here:

- ....

- ....

- ....

- ....
- ....

Reading Tracker

Book title: ....

Author: ....

Date finished: .... Score out of 10 ☐

Book title: ....

Author: ....

Date finished: .... Score out of 10 ☐

Book title: ....

Author: ....

Date finished: .... Score out of 10 ☐

Book title: ....

Author: ....

Date finished: .... Score out of 10 ☐

Book title: ....

Author: ....

Date finished: .... Score out of 10 ☐

Book title: ....

Author: ....

Date finished: .... Score out of 10 ☐

Book title: ....

Author: ....

Date finished: .... Score out of 10 ☐

Book title: ....

Author: ....

Date finished: .... Score out of 10 ☐

Book title: ....

Author: ....

Date finished: .... Score out of 10 ☐

Book title: ....

Author: ....

Date finished: .... Score out of 10 ☐

Read-alikes

If you liked *Under My Feet*,
why not try ...

Tales from Outer Suburbia
by Shaun Tan

In Focus
by Libby Walden

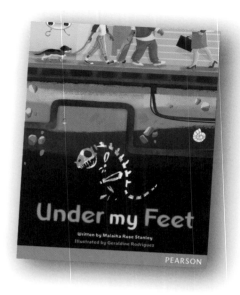

If you liked *The King in the Car Park*,
why not try ...

Horrible Histories: Terrible Tudors
by Terry Deary and Neil Tonge

Kings and Queens
by Tony Robinson

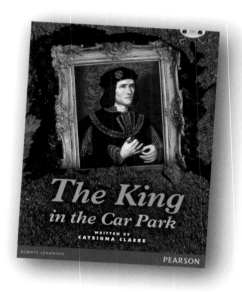

If you liked *Below Deck: A Titanic Story*,
why not try ...

Story of the Titanic
by DK and Steve Noon

You wouldn't want to sail on the Titanic!
by David Stewart

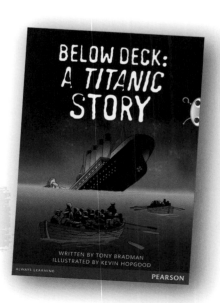

The types of text I have read this term

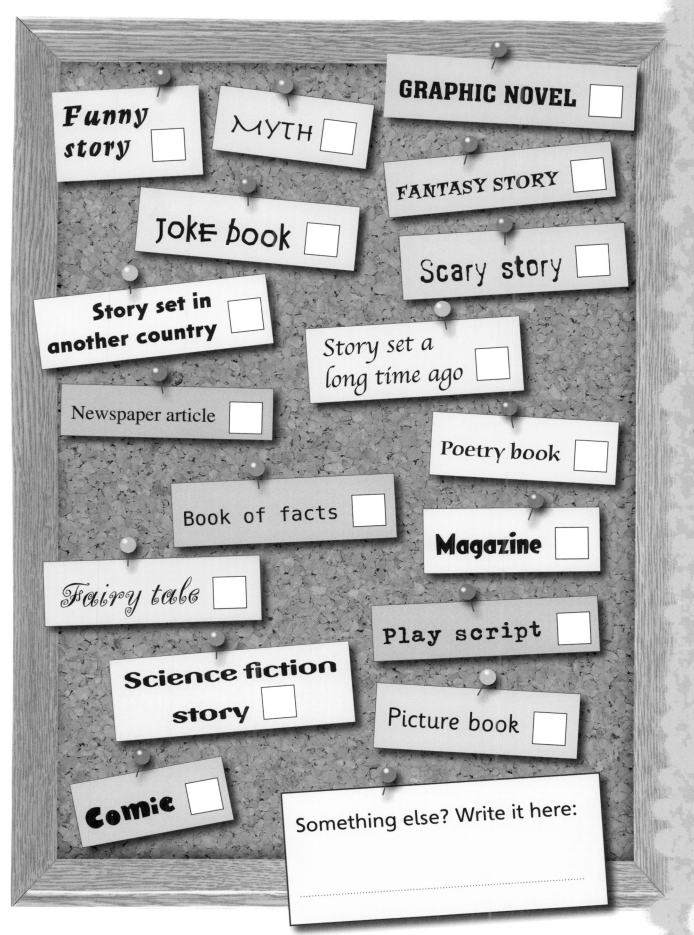

Funny story ☐

MYTH ☐

GRAPHIC NOVEL ☐

FANTASY STORY ☐

JOKE book ☐

Scary story ☐

Story set in another country ☐

Story set a long time ago ☐

Newspaper article ☐

Poetry book ☐

Book of facts ☐

Magazine ☐

Fairy tale ☐

Play script ☐

Science fiction story ☐

Picture book ☐

Comic ☐

Something else? Write it here:

....

The best new words I have learned this term

Word	What it means
osteologist	Scientist who studies bones

The best jokes I have read this term

What did Richard III say when a proposal for building a car park was submitted?

"Over my dead body!"

Reading Record

Fill in these sheets for one story you have chosen yourself.

At the beginning

Title:

Author:

Why did you choose this book?

What score do you think you'll give it? ⬚ /10

Who is the character you like most?

Has anything like this ever happened to you?

What questions do you have about the story?

What do you think will happen at the end?

At the end

Were your predictions right?

Is there anything that still puzzles you?

What score would you give this book? /10

Who do you think would enjoy this book?

The best facts I have read this term

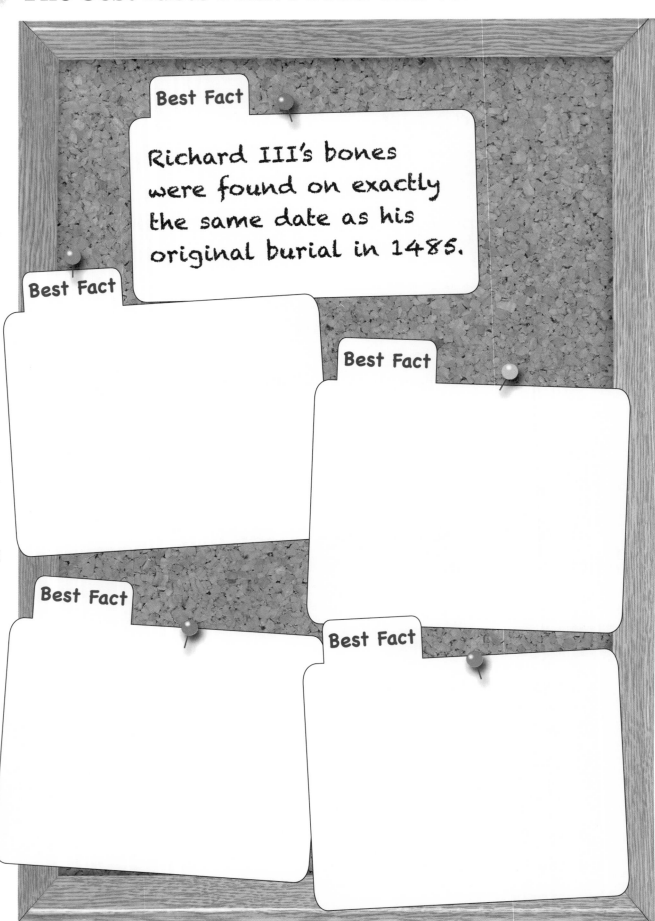

Best Fact

Richard III's bones were found on exactly the same date as his original burial in 1485.

Best Fact

Best Fact

Best Fact

Best Fact

Recommended Reads for Me

Think about someone in your group, class or family. What books would you recommend for them?

Recommended Reads for

A story I think they'll like:

A non-fiction book I think they'll like:

A poem I think they'll like:

An author I think they'll like:

What books have been recommended for you? Write them here.

Bug Club Comprehension is a fresh new approach that helps every child master comprehension. It uses a powerful and proven talk-based, mastery approach to help children develop a deeper understanding of texts.

Part of the Bug Club Comprehension programme, the workbooks provide:

- activities for each day of the teaching cycle
- clear, child-friendly designs that complement the accompanying texts
- formative assessment opportunities
- a 'Reading Journal' section for children to record their independent reading.

Series Consultants:
Wayne Tennent and David Reedy
Workbook and Teaching Card Authors:
Catherine Casey, Sarah Snashall and Andy Taylor

Published by Pearson Education Limited, 80 Strand, London, WC2R 0RL.

www.pearsonschools.co.uk

Text © Pearson Education Limited 2017

Designed by Karen Awadzi, Red Giraffe
Original illustrations © Pearson Education Limited 2017
Illustrated by Geraldine Rodriguez and Kevin Hopgood

First published 2017

21 20 19 18
10 9 8 7 6

British Library Cataloguing in Publication Data
A catalogue record for this book is available from the British Library

ISBN 978 0 435 18590 9

Printed in the UK by Ashford Colour Press.

Acknowledgements
The publisher would like to thank the following for their kind permission to reproduce their photographs in this workbook and accompanying photocopiable activities:

123RF.com: 12tl; **Alamy Images:** Classic Image 12cl, GL Archive 10, 26, PCM_10, PCM_9, Hulton Archive 12c, Trinity Mirror / Mirrorpix 25; **Shutterstock.com:** aquariagirl1970 12bl, Jane Rix 12l, Morgan Lane Photography 12br, Robbi 56, 62; **University of Leicester:** 12tr

Cover images: *Front:* **Alamy Images:** epa european pressphoto agency b.v.

All other images © Pearson Education

www.pearsonschools.co.uk
enquiries@pearson.com

ISBN 978-0-435-18590-9

9 780435 185909